For Braylon, the one thing in this world
that keeps me motivated, determined and
driven for more.
Mommy loves you my sweet baby boy!

Boutique Image Consulting & Personal Branding Firm

Dolcé Belletto

PO Box 632

Antioch, TN 37011

www.dolcebelletto.com

info@dolcebelletto.com

615-375-6483

Follow us on Twitter : @DolceBelletto

Like us on Facebook: www.facebook.com/dolcebelletto

Join our group on LinkedIn:

http://www.linkedin.com/groups/Dolce-Belletto-Branding-Image-Consulting-5124421

ABOUT THE AUTHOR

Contrecia Tharpe is an award nominated brand and image strategist. With over 5 years' experience in the entertainment industry, she works with entertainers, athletes, politicians and small businesses on brand development, brand management, brand positioning, image, visual presentation and maintaining a brand and image that is cohesive, clear and consistent …what she calls 'completing the trifecta of success' . She has spoken at seminars, given webinars, sat on panels, contributed on blogs and worked hand in hand with personalities around the nation. *Branding Blocks: A Guide to Developing a Brand and Image for Success* is her first published work as an author. She lives in Nashville, Tennessee with her son Braylon.

www.linkedin.com/in/contreciatharpe
www.contreciatharpe.com

Table of Contents

Chapter 1:

Introduction

"Success is creating a plan and implementing it!"

INTRODUCTION

When I started my first business, over 18 years ago at the age of 10, my ultimate goal was to be successful and to make as many friendship bracelets, key chains and accessories as possible. With my cousin, we went into business as TNT and started selling accessories to anyone who was willing to purchase our little creative concoctions. At the time, success was measured by the constant purchasing of string and the orders that came in....until everyone learned to do what we were doing and began to make their own accessories out of string. That is where most businesses, entrepreneurs and individuals are today. They are struggling to remain relevant as the 'go to' in industries that have become over populated with people who believe that 1.) They can do it themselves, 2.) They can do it just as good as or better than the current options presented or 3.) They see the success another person has and wants to obtain that same success at a different cost. Either way, in a world full of people that do your exact craft, you have to ask yourself 'How can I stand out?'... 'How can I make myself, my brand and my image unique?'

WHAT IS SUCCESS?

Success is defined as the accomplishment of an aim or purpose; however, some definitions refer to success as the attainment of popularity, profit and/or wealth. Regardless of the definition, success is something each individual craves and desires to obtain at some point in life. Many are lost as to what steps they need to take in order to reach their ultimate goal(s). 'Where do I start?' is a general question about success and that is the purpose of this book. Brand-Aid is a guide to start understanding the development of your brand and image so that your offering, as a whole, is one that travels the path to success smoothly. When paired with the Brand-Aid activities at the end of each chapter, they collectively assist in laying out the fundamental elements of your image and brand.

Success is the bigger picture composed of smaller pieces. It is an equation composed of image, branding, profession, career, art or talent and marketing all targeted towards a specific demographic. If you take one piece of the equation and only work on that part, your total (success) will never reach the potential that it could. You will always fall shorter than if you had implemented and worked on each component of the equation. Brand Aid guides you towards a solid development of your brand and image in totality instead of each unit alone.

WHAT IS YOUR GAUGE OF SUCCESS?

When will you be able to determine that your efforts have not been in vain? It will not be instantaneous, it is a process. It could be weeks, months, years or decades...the timeframe is based on your personal definition of success. For some, it's reaching 50k followers on social media, for others it may be the ability to purchase their dream car. Some base success off of visuals…we believe what we see, what we can touch, what is tangible. If it looks successful, then it must be successful. Some measure it solely by their brand. If their brand is known, even in the midst of a scandal, they are pleased. 'All publicity is good publicity' has become a common metaphor for brands today. If people are discussing the brand, then it has to be successful.

It is important to understand what your ideal and envisioned success entails. By having a clear idea of what your success looks like or consists of, then you will be able to plan your goals to achieve those results.

DO YOU HAVE A PLAN?

Success requires careful planning and outlining of current, short-term and long term goals. From those goals that you set, you can lay out a blueprinted guideline and time line to help you recognize resources needed, deadlines/timeframes, individuals you need around you to assist in getting certain tasks done and prioritize goals in either sequential order or order of importance. Goal setting and planning is the most important part of brand development. How can you know where you want to end up, if you don't know the road to take that leads there? Without intention or planning, goals go unachieved.

In any successful brand or image, a plan is essential and necessary. It is also important to continuously analyze your plans for accurate and up-to-date measures of completion rates and success. When outlining your plan, you should, first, understand the difference between goals, objectives and

WHAT IS YOUR GAUGE OF SUCCESS?

tactics/strategies. Your goals are your broad, abstract intentions. They are the general direction that you are headed. Objectives are more concrete, narrow and precise measures used to obtain or reach an achievement. Tactics are strategies and methods to be used to obtain the objectives and the goals. For example, your goal is to buy a home. Your objectives would be to pay off credit card debt, find a home and a mortgage broker. While your tactics, would be paying $200 a month on credit card debt until debt is $0, finding a mortgage broker with a loan product that has a 3.9% fixed rate or less and a home that has 3 bedrooms and 3.5 bathrooms in the southern portion of the city.

To many, this may seem extreme and complete overkill, but this type of detail allows you to create a thorough blueprint for your brand and image.

WHAT TO EXPECT FROM THIS BOOK

This book will help you gain an intermediate level understanding of branding and image as it relates to your market, career and goals. At the end of every chapter there will be action plans and activities/tasks for you to complete that correlates with the material you just read. By the time you reach the end of this book, you should have outlined and established a strong starting point to begin developing your brand and image! Ready. Set. Plan!

Note: I recommend getting a 3 subject notebook to complete the activities in. With a 3 subject notebook, you can set a tab for branding, image and notes. This allows you to place all information and plans in one location and refer back to it with ease. Try to find a notebook that does not have perforated pages...this helps eliminate the desire to tear pages out and keeps your plans and ideas intact.

ACTION PLAN

- complete activities for Chapter 1

ACTIVITIES

All About You
Name:
Stage Name: (if applicable)
Career/Industry:
Length in Field:
Social Media Links/User ID

-Twitter:
-Facebook Business Page:
-Pinterest:
-LinkedIn:
-YouTube:
Website(s):

Blog URL(s):

Chapter 2:

What is a Brand?

"Your brand is the property you own in the mind of your target market"

WHAT IS A BRAND?

According to Wikipedia, a brand is the "name, term, design, symbol, or any other feature that identifies one seller's product from others". Let's rework this definition to better suit you. Let's remove the phrase 'one seller's product' and replace it with 'you'. Let's replace 'symbol' with 'logo' and 'design' with 'visual presentation'. From this, we can gather that a brand is the development of characteristics, features and traits that differentiate you from the others in your industry. Your brand is your face in the marketplace and the message that you want to push to your target market.

As stated by Francis Somuah, your brand is the powerful, clear, positive idea that comes to mind whenever people think of you. It is what you stand for-the values, abilities, beliefs and actions that others associate with you. It is the impression you create; the mental picture or idea that is formed based on your actions or inactions.

A solid and clear brand helps:
- define who you are
- associate great value with your product (which can be yourself), service, offering and/or craft
- build demand for your talents, services and skills
- increase awareness and visibility
- market yourself
- create uniqueness and recognition
- establish you in your target market

But let's be clear. Your brand is not just one part of what you do or who you are, it is the totality of your essence

21

and abilities as a person. It's your entity's DNA and the imprint you leave in your demographics' mind. Your brand is verbal and non-verbal communication…it's your message-seen, heard, interpreted and translated by the public.

You will often see postings asking 'What does your brand say about you?' This phrase is asking you to analyze what message your brand is conveying to your consumer base. Is it a message that speaks highly of your product, service, offering or craft? Does it clearly identify who you are and what you stand for? Does it connect and link with your vision and mission statements? Does it clearly show your morals and beliefs in business? Does it differentiate you from others in your industry? Is your brand too similar to others? Is it loud or is it quiet? Does it showcase you as an expert or as a rookie? Does it have a professional presentation? The questions could go on and on and to accurately answer them, you would need to understand the characteristics and components of a successful brand.

CHARACTERISTICS OF A SUCCESSFUL BRAND

As with everything in business, you have to cultivate your brand so that, if it has to stand on its own, it speaks well of you in every way. There are certain qualities and traits that every brand should have regardless of the industry:

- **Relatablity**: Does your brand speak to the audience that you are trying to attract? Is there something in your brand that your target market either 1) sees in themselves; or 2) desires to be? Your brand is your way to connect to your market through your vision, mission, beliefs and craft/career/passion. Can your audience relate to what you are doing?

- **Clear:** Is your brand's identity and message clear to your audience? Can your message easily be misconstrued or confusing? Is it simple enough to engage, yet clear enough to explain? Throughout the transitions of business, your mission and message can become blurred. It is important to always maintain a clear and concise message with your brand.

- **Consistent:** Is your brand's presentation reliable and similar regardless of the situation or environment? Consumers are typically more comfortable with a brand that they can trust and who appears the same a majority of the time...if not all the time. By remaining consistent, you show your audience that you are confident in your offering and sure of who you are as a brand and a person.

- **Cohesive:** Does your brand tie in with everything that you have going on? Your brand should match and align with every part of your entity/product/service. It should match your image, your mission, your market, your vision and your offering. Think of each piece as a brick, without the mortar they can't properly serve their purpose.

- **Flexible:** The wise Heraclitus once said 'Nothing is constant but change' and he could not have been more right. In a world, where change happens every day, your brand has to be able to maintain its identity and consumer loyalty. As your audience's preference(s) change, so must your brand...while remaining clear, consistent, cohesive and relatable. You must constantly tweak your brand to make sure it is as up to date as possible. Your brand is never finished; it is a constant progression that changes as you, the market and the world changes.

- **Uniqueness:** Does your brand speak of you as an individual or you as a cookie cutter copy of another individual/entity in the industry? Is your market able to decipher you from others doing the same thing as you? Do you stand out enough to draw attention, yet fit in enough to retain consumer loyalty? This is the era for the unique brand and individual. Allow your brand to showcase you as an individual instead of showcasing you as just a puzzle piece to a bigger puzzle. You want your brand to be its own enigma that is found in the industry... if that makes sense.

- **Passionate:** If you are not passionate about your brand, then why should anyone buy into or support it? Your brand reflects how you feel about and the confidence you have in it. People are easily able to determine if this is something you love to do or if this is just something you are doing to fill an income void in your life. Your brand should showcase the love you have for the industry. People should look at your brand and see that you are happy to be offering them your product(s) and/or service(s). Studies show that people are more willing to buy into what you are doing, when they see you are intensely enthusiastic and serious about what you are doing.

WHAT DOES YOUR BRAND SAY ABOUT YOU?

COMPONENTS OF A SUCCESSFUL BRAND

Now that the characteristics and traits of a successful brand have been listed, we need to discuss the components of a brand. This is a primary list of things that you need in order begin branding yourself. The list will be discussed more in Chapter 5.

- **Purpose:** Your purpose is why you are here and and what you are here to be. It establishes the reasons you have entered the market.
- **Mission:** Your mission is what you are here to accomplish. It states the goal, tasks and actions desired to take. Many people combine the purpose and the mission together. In fact, many mission statements begin with 'our purpose is to...'
- **Vision:** What you see for your business and the market attached to your business. It is what you en*vision* as possible for your brand/business
- **Values/Beliefs:** What you value most in your brand, business, experience and market. It is the worth that you see and wants others to see in your brand.

- **Logo:** A logo is a symbol or design that identifies one brand from another. Be clear that your logo is NOT your brand; it is just an identifying feature of your brand. Many sources suggest having variations of your logo: 1.) your main image, 2.) your image and brand/business name and 3.) Your image, brand/business name and tag line. Below are the list of logo types:
  - **Textual Logo:** These are distinctively designed logos that showcase the brand's name. Examples are Coca Cola, Disney and Subway.
  - **Symbolic Logo:** These are logos that are easily identifiable by a specific symbol. Examples are Shell Gas Station, Facebook, Twitter, Nike, Cadillac and Prince.
  - **Letter Logo:** These logos are created with the initials of a company. Examples are HP (Hewlett Packard), DB (Dolce

Belletto) and Chanel's interlocked C's.

- o **Combination Logo:** This logo is a combination of a symbolic logo and a textual logo. Examples are Verizon and Adidas.
- o **Emblem Logo:** An emblem logo showcases the brand's name within the logo design. Examples are the NFL and Starbucks.

THINGS TO TAKE INTO CONSIDERATION WITH YOUR BRAND

Your brand is a representation of you at all times. It is your non-verbal communication when you cannot speak to your market personally. Because of this, you have to make sure that the message that your brand is sending is an accurate portrayal of you. You must also analyze other brands in the industry and see the similarities. Are you an identical brand to someone else? It is okay to possess similar traits, but avoid being a carbon copy. It is okay to assess what has made your competition successful and implement those strategies that work best for you and your market into your plan; however, I do not suggest copying your competition's brand completely. By becoming a spitting image of them, you will label yourself as a 'copycat' or be known as 'the brand like X, but they are not X'. You never want someone to be more drawn to your competition because they are not able to separate the two. Uniqueness is key.

DEMOGRAPHIC

You also need to take your target market into consideration. Who is your client/ consumer base? What market will respond to your brand's vision, mission, values beliefs, purpose and ideas? There are methods used to determine your target market that we will touch on in Chapter 5.

FLEXIBILITY AND LIFE SPAN OF INDUSTRY

In creating a brand, especially if this is something that you plan on committing yourself to for a length of time, it is IMPORTANT to consider if the industry and your brand is flexible. Is it something that you can nurture, improve and grow overtime or is it an industry/brand with a shelf life that will soon expire? You should make sure that your brand is able to bend and move as the industry's climate changes. Your brand should be able to grow with your target consumer base. An example of failed brand flexibility are musicians who craft their brand solely on their consumers are in that very moment with little regard to who their consumers will become in the future. Ask yourself how some artists are able to stay in the industry for decades at a time? They either:

1.) Grow and change their brand as their demographic changes and grows. As their audience matures, their lyrical content changes to suit the consumer's new mind set, or,

2.) They alter their brand and image to be able to market themselves to a different demographic who will still appreciate their unchanged craft.

Whichever option they choose, they created a brand that could be changed to fit the environment of their industry at any point. A flexible brand is a brand that can sustain the test of time and still remain relevant. Apple is a flexible brand...technology is an ever-changing industry and Apple continues to change its brand while remaining true to its original mission, vision and values. The company has not changed, the brand and the image has changed to cope with the fast paced industry it is in.

MARKET TRENDS

Constantly analyze your competition's brand, your own brand and market trends. By staying on top of the industry, research wise, you are able to maintain a solid brand and presence. Your brand should never be a finished product; it is a process, so expect to constantly fine-tune, update and/or change your message.

BRANDING TERMS

- **Branding:** the development of the elements, components and characteristics that differentiate and identify you from direct & indirect competition.
- **Brand Strategy:** creating a plan for the development of a strong, cohesive, clear and consistent brand in order to enhance awareness, revenue, profits and successful completion of goals and objectives; should be driven by the principles of differentiation and target market appeal.

- **Brand Positioning:** the placement and position that a brand takes in its industry to ensure that their target market can differentiate between it and others in the industry.
- **Brand Loyalty:** the degree that an individual in the target market is committed to a given brand. The level of brand loyalty is a clear indication of how protected a brand is from its competition.
- **Brand Awareness:** the amount of people (either in numbers or percentages) within a target market that are aware of the existence of a brand.
- **Brand Definition:** the essence of who, what and why a brand is; its mission, vision, purpose and values.
- **Brand Management:** analyzing of a brand to determine positioning, target market and how to maintain/manage the brand's reputation. Creating and maintaining a good rapport with your target market is necessary for success.

- **Brand Identity:** the perception of a brand gathered by its visual presentation, image and its name; differentiates the brand from others and help target consumers to recognize the brand. What a brand looks like - including, among other things, its logo, typography and color choices.
- **Core Competencies:** areas of skill and strength that a brand possesses (Chapter 5)
- **Demographic:** the description of outward traits that characterize a group of people, such as age, sex, lifestyle, nationality, marital status, place of residence, education, occupation or income
- **Differentiation:** creation or demonstration of unique characteristics in brands compared to those of its competitors.
- **Rebranding:** revisiting of the brand with the purpose of updating or revising it based on internal or external circumstances. Rebranding is often necessary if the brand has outgrown its identity/marketplace.

ACTION PLAN

- Research industry; you want to become an expert in your field regardless of what it is. Constant education is key!!
- Research indirect and direct competition; you want to know what they are doing, if they are succeeding, who their target market is, what their niche is and what methods/tactics they are implementing.
- Set up google alerts for your industry, competition and your brand. Google Alerts is a service offered by Google that emails you once a day with new articles, blog posts or other finding on Google on your selected topics.
  - go to www.google.com/alerts
  - type in keywords or phrases
  - select your frequency
  - choose the email address you want them delivered to
- Complete Chapter 2 Activities

ACTIVITIES

What are you going to brand? (Service, product, yourself, etc) (list everything that you are doing, we will revisit this list in Chapter 5's activities):

Who is currently doing what you are doing or something similar?

Where is your competitor(s) located? Is it in the same region or areas as you?

Whose career do you wish to model yours after? What is their website(s)? Social Media links or usernames?:

Brand Checklist (check of the things that you currently have, make note of the things that you do not. We will revisit this in Chapter 5's activities):

- ☐ Logo
- ☐ Twitter Page
- ☐ Facebook Page
- ☐ YouTube
- ☐ LinkedIn
- ☐ Google+
- ☐ Website
- ☐ Business Cards
- ☐ Fliers
- ☐ Brochures (services and product industries only)

Do you want to be an endorsed brand? (Have someone else represent your brand) If so, who and why?

List reasons why are you here, what are you here to be and what you are here to do. We will include this into a mission/ purpose statement in Chapter 5.

List what you wish to see for your business. We will turn this into a vision statement in Chapter 5.

Brainstorm:

☐ Product (what you are offering and how are you different than the competition)

☐ Beliefs (values that guide you)

☐ Actions (what are you willing to do to get you to the end result you desire)

☐ Benefits (what is the benefit of choosing you over the competition)

Chapter 3

What is Image?

*"**Image and perception help drive value; without an image, there is no perception**"*

-Scott M. Davis

WHAT IS IMAGE?

Webster's Dictionary defines image as a mental picture; the thought of how something looks or might look; the idea that people have about someone or something. Image is a representation of the external form of a person. It is the general impression that someone presents to the public. How you appear to others, especially those in your target market, is important...as the saying goes, "There is never a second chance to make a first impression". Our visual presentation (grooming and clothing) and outward appearance determines 95%of first impressions. In the first FOUR SECONDS of meeting you, most people have judged you. That judgment is finalized in the next THIRTY SECONDS. The CFP (Certified Financial Planners) Board

41

has a commercial out where they transformed a DJ into a pseudo-CFP. They reconstructed his image and had him meet with several potential clients. Based off of his image, those clients believed that he was a genuine financial planner. This commercial demonstrates the power of a strong image that aligns with your career, talent or craft.

Your image is not just based on your clothing and grooming. It also consists of several other elements including your tone of voice, vocabulary, facial expressions, eye contact, non-verbal gestures and social etiquette. Your behavior and presentation, as a whole, has the ability to affect or change how someone views you, your talent and your brand. A person's perception of a trait typically leads to other thoughts and assumptions, or lack thereof, of an individual. For example, a person who is well-dressed is typically deemed as successful and wealthy. A person who articulates well is typically deemed as educated. One who makes eye contact is seen as confident and secure. For this book, we will focus on the grooming, clothing and visual presentation of your image. Your image is a key factor people weigh when you all interact.

Image is a component of success that most people neglect or forget all together; however, it is just as important as your offering and brand. It rounds out the trifecta which consists of your brand, your image and your offering.

CHARACTERISTICS OF A SUCCESSFUL IMAGE

In order to develop an image that aids in your success, you must first understand what your image must possess.

A successful image is:

- **Uniquely Identifiable**: Does your image differentiate you from your competition? Are there traits of your image that are unique to you? For example, Nicki Minaj coined the bright colored makeup in the urban music industry, Rick Ross coined the beard and Lady Gaga is known for outrageous fashion. This allows people to familiarize themselves with your visual

> THERE IS NEVER A SECOND CHANCE TO MAKE A FIRST IMPRESSION

presentation and usually leads them to research you more because of the visual attraction or appeal. However, keep in mind that your uniqueness must be simple enough to be instantly and easily recognized. It is not necessary to make your image a visual replica of your brand, but to make your image a visual representation of the message that you want your brand to say, therefore complementing your brand. If your image is a visual replica you run the risk of it being too similar or exactly like your competition.

- **Pleasing and Appealing:** Is your image appealing to your target market? You have to create an image that complements your brand, your personality and is visually attractive to and draws in your target market. This requires that you research your target market, their likes and dislikes. Color also plays a large part into the appeal of your visual image. Some color choices can deter customers.

- **Memorable:** Does your image make you, as a whole, memorable? After your interaction with a person or group, are you and the impression you left still on their mind or does it quickly fade? The goal is to draw people in so that you are able to create a positive lasting impression. Positive lasting impressions increases brand loyalty, word of mouth and future dealings.
- **Culturally and Demographically Respectful:** Colors, gestures and clothing have different meanings in various cultures. You do not want your image to be offensive to a portion of your demographic because of a lack of knowledge on cultural differences. Research your demographic thoroughly to avoid offending those you are trying to reach or attract.
- **Flexible:** Your image should be able to change as your brand and demographic changes. As you mature, gain more experience, change markets or grow your market, your image should be able to keep

up with each and every demand. As with your brand, your image will continue to require adjusting and updating.

- **Consistent:** Your image should be able to translate into an activity or event that you participate in or attend. It is essential to establish an image that can work in any environment. Whether you are at a professional meeting, a gala or a casual networking party, your image should consistently fall into your chosen style. Cultivate a style and image that you are comfortable and familiar with so that consistency is not an issue.

- **Clear:** Your image should be a clear representation of your brand, message and career. Your intentions with your image should be concise. It should be clear why you are unique!

- **Cohesive:** Your image should cohesively complete your trifecta. It should relate to your career/profession/craft/talent and brand in a complementary way. For example, your image should not be that of a rapper, your message about the importance of car insurance and your demographic is children under the age of 10. One has nothing to do with the other. Make sure that your image connects the dots and aligns with everything else you are presenting.

- **Well Put Together:** Your brand should be neat in appearance, even when going for the messy look. It is important to have an order to your execution. Order and neatness are necessary for a professional presentation.

THINGS TO TAKE INTO CONSIDERATION WITH YOUR IMAGE

When you are developing your brand, you have to take your demographic, body shape, brand, offering and color choices into consideration.

DEMOGRAPHIC

Your demographic should definitely affect your decision making when it comes to your image. You should consider what is appealing to them, trends that they currently are following, what is offensive to them and how they view style and fashion. In order to appeal to your market, you have to understand and know what your market likes and looks for in brands from your industry.

BODY SHAPE

It is easy to fall into the current trends of fashion, but you must be careful. You must search out an image and style that is fitting for your body shape. Be mindful of how clothing fits your body. Clothing designers and manufacturers offer various cuts to compliment different body shapes, types and sizes. Before making a purchase, it is a great idea to research cuts and which style of clothing looks best on your body type.

For women, depending on the demographic you desire to market yourself to, be aware, at all times, of the parts of your body you are accentuating. Low cut shirts, short skirts and clothing inappropriate for a particular environment send the wrong message. A professional image is one that gains more respect. You never want people to assume that your success came from the type of clothing you wear.

BRAND AND CRAFT/PROFESSION/CAREER

We have stated several times that your image should complement your brand and what you are offering to the market. By taking these things into consideration when developing your image, you are able to create an extremely solid total package. Keep in mind the statement from earlier about avoiding a brand replica and implementing a brand representation with your image.

COLOR CHOICES

Colors can mean different things to different people. Colors can also affect the way you feel in a particular outfit. This is the reason that we see many people in a certain color repeatedly. Various shades of blue and red, black and white are very popular and common color choices. Neutral colors also rank high on the color choice list. Be fully aware of color choice and how they many affect the opinion of your demographic.

You also want to choose colors that complement your skin tone well. In order to do so, you will need to determine if you have a warm, neutral or cool undertone to your skin. We will do this in Chapter 6 when we breakdown the development of your image one component at a time.

ACTION PLAN:

- Research style types
- Research competition's image
- Research various body types
- Research which cut of clothing fits whit body type
- Complete Activities for Chapter 3

ACTIVITIES:

Whose style does you like and why?

What trends do you currently like?

What current trends would you eliminate if you could?

What is your competition's image?

Monthly Image Stipend (Realistic):

- Hair/Grooming: _____

- Makeup/Beauty: _____

- Clothing: _____

- Shoes: _____

Total/Month: _____

What is visually appealing to you?

What are your favorite colors?

Chapter 4:

Why is a Brand and

Image Important?

"Your brand and image is the distinctive identity that sets you apart from others in the same market place."

WHY IS A BRAND AND IMAGE IMPORTANT?

When we learn how to analyze a story at an early age, we are taught to identify who, what, when, where, how and why so that we can accurately assess the message and tone of the book. The same methods are used when people evaluate your brand and image. Your brand and image tells the public who you are, what you do and plan to do, why you plan to do it, how you plan to do it and who you are doing it for, among other things.

There are several reasons why your brand and image are important; these two round out the trifecta that you must have for success. The trifecta, which you have read about in previous chapters, consists of your brand, your image and your offering. A total package that is cohesive and appeals to your target market increases awareness and provides a solid foundation for success to be built on. The more solid the foundation, the more stable your success!

Having a strong image and brand presentation that interrelates with your offering also creates a higher value of you as an entity and generates new business and a following. It is more difficult to attract new consumers/clients/listeners/fans than it is to retain those that are already familiar and supportive of you. A brand and image that is created with your offering in mind and tailored to a market, helps you stand out in a crowd and increases the likelihood of brand loyalty. You are not a monopoly; there are several people

> # THE MORE SOLID THE FOUNDATION, THE MORE STABLE YOUR SUCCESS!

doing exactly what you are doing…you MUST stand out. For example, in the fast food restaurant business you have several options with McDonald's, Burger King, Wendy's,

Krystal's...they each have the same objective and business offering which is to serve food at a faster pace to people on the go; however, each brand/entity has established themselves from their competition. This is the purpose of having a brand and image that is your own!

Remember, what you do matters, how you do it is important and why you do it is critical!

ACTION PLAN AND ACTIVITIES:

There are no action plan and activities for this chapter. Beginning with Chapter 5, we will begin developing your brand and image. Your Action Plan and Activities will fall

#OWNYOURBRAND

#OWNYOURIMAGE

after each section of the chapters instead of at the end. We will work in a calculated way to research, map out and develop a plan to get you to your success!

Chapter 5:

Developing Your Brand

"What you do

+ Who you do it for

+How you are unique

= You: The Brand"

DEVELOPING YOUR BRAND

In this chapter, we will begin to put together the components of your brand. At the end of chapter 2, you completed several activities to get you thinking about what you want your brand to consists of and possess. You researched your competition's brand and looked at the way their entities were set up; you also researched the industry that you are in or want to house your new business entity. With those building blocks, we can begin to build your brand.

TARGET MARKET

Your target market is the group of individuals that you decide to aim your marketing and branding efforts towards. A well-defined target market is the first step in a solid brand strategy.

You will need to break down the demographic based on certain information. Let's complete the table below; you can use www.sba.gov/content/demographics or www.pewresearch.org to look up information. You can also utilize the research you did on your industry and competition to help in making some of the decisions. It is not necessary to target the same demographic as your competition, there could be a niche (read: specialized) market that is currently being overlooked. You can also conduct a survey for people to fill out that gives you more of an inside look at your demographic!

You base your choices in the following activity off of who you believe will support your profession, craft, talent or career. It is easy to say that you want everyone to be your target market, but you cannot be everything to everybody. You need to narrow down your choices so that you can develop a total package that is appealing to your market!

ACTIVITY:

Category	Targeted Choices
Age : What is the age range that your target market falls into? Why this market?	
Location: What area(s) does your target market currently reside? Why this area?	
Race: What ethnic background(s) does your target market belong to?	
Gender(s):	
Income Level: What income range does your target market bring in solely? Their household?	
Education Level:	

What is the highest level of education completed for your target market?	
Marital Status: Is your target market married, single, divorced, widowed or engaged? Or does this not matter with your offering?	
Occupation: What does your target market do for a living?	
Personal Characteristics	
Personality: Is your target market more introverted or extroverted?	
Values: What does your target market believe in?	
Interests/hobbies: What does your target market do for fun? Where do they hang	

out?	
Behavior: What is your target market's consumer behavior? What do they support? Who is big in your industry among this demographic?	

Now that you have broken down your target demographic, let's see if you broke it down too far.

Question	Answer
Are there enough people that fit your criteria? *This can be found by looking at census.gov information for this area.*	
Will your target really benefit from your offering? Will they see a need for it?	

Do you understand what drives your target market to make decisions? If yes, what drives them? If no, research consumer trends for your industry.	
Can your target market afford your product/service/art? (if this applies)	
Can you reach them with your message? Are they easily accessible?	

You can have more than one niche market, but keep in mind that your marketing approach and message will have to change. This can increase marketing cost greatly; I highly recommend conquering one market at a time when starting out.

BRAND DEFINITION:
MISSION/PURPOSE:

A mission statement is defined by Google as "a formal summary of the aims and values of a company, organization, or individual.". It establishes who you are, what you do and your purpose. At the end of chapter 2, you wrote down why are you here, what are you here to be and what you are here to do. Now that we have determined your target market, we can take this and turn it into your mission/purpose statement.

In order to turn your answers into a mission statement, there are a few more questions to answer.

Question	Answer

MISSION STATEMENT HELP CLARIFY WHAT BUSINESS YOU ARE IN, YOUR GOALS AND YOUR OBJECTIVES"
- RHONDA ABRAMS

Why are you in business? What do you want for yourself, your family and your customers? Think about the spark that ignited your decision to start a business. What will keep it burning?	
Who are your customers? What can you do for them that will enrich their lives and contribute to their success--now and in the future?	
What image of your business do you want to convey? The public will all have perceptions of your company. How will you create the desired picture?	

How do you differ from your competitors? Many entrepreneurs forget they are pursuing the same dollars as their competitors. What do you do better, cheaper or faster than other competitors? How can you use competitors' weaknesses to your advantage?

What underlying philosophies or values guided your responses to the previous questions? Some businesses choose to list these separately. Writing them

down clarifies the "why" behind your mission.	

**Questions provided by Entrepreneur.com, 2003*

Your mission statement's length depends on the message you want to give to the public. It can long or short... it's up to you. Below are a few sample mission statements:

To remember where I have been and where I will go through maintaining positive relationships with family and friends. To choose the ethical way by making a personal commitment to honesty and integrity. To find peacefulness within myself by looking inward while using my heart to guide my dreams and desires, and my mind to pursue knowledge, creating balance among all of my obligations. To content myself in my surroundings so I will always know where security lies within my life. To build a reputation of being dedicated to every goal I choose to pursue while having successes in both my personal and professional life. To enjoy every moment along this journey finding laughter, love, and happiness with each day that passes. – Digital Portfolio

My mission in life is to serve God by being: A beacon of light, A bridge of understanding, A tower of integrity, and A castle of realized dreams. –Touchpoint Coaching

Our goal is to position Zappos as the online service leader. If we can get customers to associate the Zappos brand with the absolute best service, then we can expand into other product categories beyond shoes. – Zappos

The mission we serve as Twitter, Inc. is to give everyone the power to create and share ideas and information instantly without barriers. Our business and revenue will always follow that mission in ways that improve–and do not detract from–a free and global conversation. –Twitter

Now it's time to put your mission statement together: My/our mission/goal/purpose is _____

_____

_____

_____

_____

_____

_____

_____

_____

_____

_____

_____

_____

If you are having issues piecing together your mission statement, visit dolcebelletto.com/missionstatement.htm# and complete the mission statement creator from missionstatements.com!

VISION STATEMENT:

Your vision statement is a lot simpler than your mission statement. It is the future that you see/ predict for you and your brand. To begin writing your vision statement, you first need to look at your mission statement. Focus on the points you made and mentioned in your mission statement and use them as motivation for your vision. Where do you see your brand and business in two years, five years? Below are some sample vision statements:

Our vision is to be earth's most customer centric company; to build a place where people can come to find and discover anything they might want to buy online. – Amazon

PepsiCo's responsibility is to continually improve all aspects of the world in which we operate - environment, social, economic - creating a better tomorrow than today. Our vision is put into action through programs and a focus on environmental stewardship, activities to benefit society, and a commitment to build shareholder value by making PepsiCo a truly sustainable company. – Pepsi Co.

What is it that you strive to be? Think in broad, long-term success for your vision. At the end of chapter 2, you answered the question "what do you wish to see for your business." We can take that and fill in your vision statement.

I/We/ Brand Name strive(s) to become/do/be _____

_____

_____

_____

_____

_____.

BRAND IDENTITY

Now that we have figured out your demographic and your mission and vision statement, we will move on to developing your brand identity. Your brand identity consists of your logo, brand name (which you may already have), color scheme and tag line.

Brand Name:	
Tag Line: Your slogan for your company; should be catchy!	
Color Scheme: What are your favorite colors? Be sure to choose colors that are complementary to each other. Complementary colors are across from each other on	

the color wheel. **See color wheel below**	

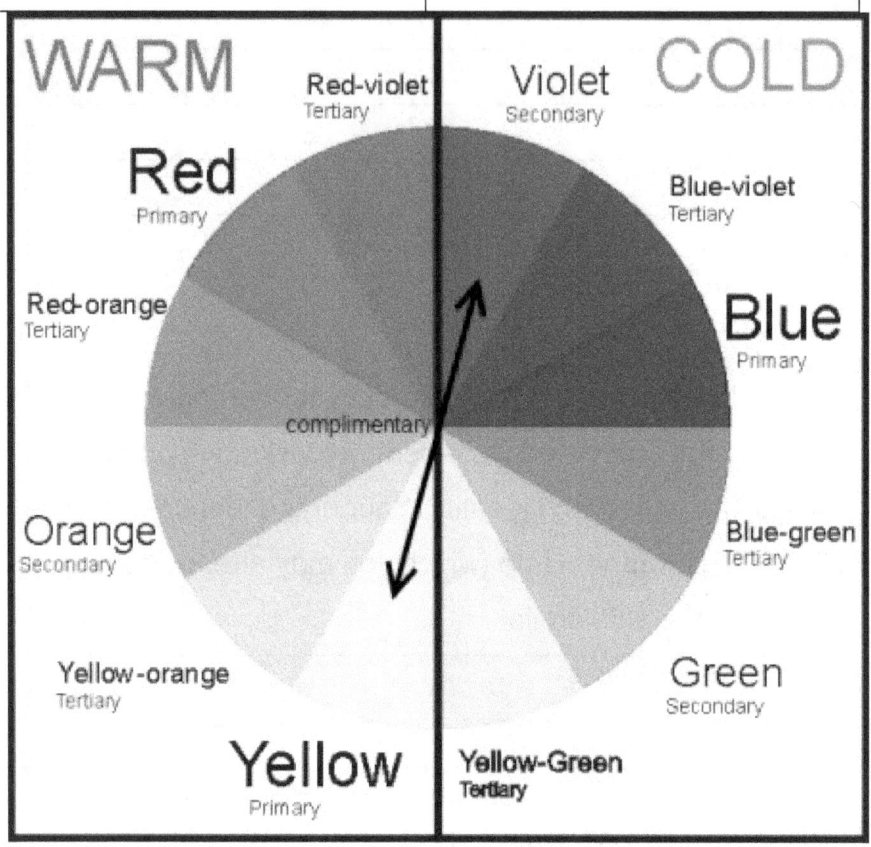

Logo Design: Choose a type of logo.	☐ Textual: distinctively designed logos that showcase the brand's name. Example: Disney. ☐ Symbolic: easily identifiable by a

	specific symbol. Example: Shell Gas. ☐ Letter: created with the initials of a company. Our logo (found on page 3) is an example. ☐ Combination: combination of a symbolic logo and a textual logo. Example: Verizon ☐ Emblem Logo: showcases the brand's name within the logo design. Example: the NFL
Begin to design your logo: What do you envision for your logo? What do you want people to see when they look at your logo? Do you want it simplistic or ornate? Avoid clipart and keep it clean and professional!	

Use this space to write down the ideas you have. ** I recommend hiring a graphic designer to create you a visual branding campaign (logo, business cards, fliers, etc.)	
Use this space to draw ideas	

SWOT ANALYSIS

A SWOT Analysis is a breakdown of your strengths, weaknesses, opportunities and threats. Your strengths and weaknesses are both internal; while opportunities and threats are external. You use this analyze to determine the best path for you to take, adjust plans, make decisions about goals and explore new possibilities.

Complete the table below.

Strengths: What are your abilities, skills and/or talents in your industry? Do you have any specific knowledge in your field? What resources do you have? Who can you ask for help? What is already working well for you in this area?	
Weaknesses: What are your main limitations? What skills/abilities are needed that you don't have? Are there any resources (money, time, help, etc.) that you need? What is not working for you in this area right now? What are you not motivated ab out?	
Opportunities:	

What opportunities have you been pursuing? Are there any opportunities presented because of your current standing?	
Threats: What external threats (changes to income, events, etc.) could affect you negatively? Are you facing any risk if you continue along your current path? What obstacles or roadblocks are in your way?	

The goal is to eliminate the weaknesses and threats and capitalize on the strengths and opportunities. We do this by creating an action plan to strengthen our core competencies and develop a plan to complete goals in a timely manner.

ACTION PLAN

An action plan is an outline of goals and objectives that need to be created. You begin with the goal, create the objectives then develop the tactics (refer to our example in chapter 1 about purchasing a home). Each element of the action plan has a completion date and should be held measureable to certain success criteria. You should perform a success assessment throughout the process to complete the action; this helps decrease the amount of time that you spend heading in the wrong direction and allows you to make necessary changes.

On the next three pages is the Dolcé Belletto Action Plan. It has five columns that allow you to create an outline:
- Action: This can be your goal, objective or tactic. I suggest filling out an action plan per goal (which is why I have included three plans to get you started). Use this column

to identify, prioritize and list goals, objectives and tactics.

- Resources: List the resources require to achieve each action.
- Time Allocated: Clearly define how long each step should take to complete.
- Deadline: Set a deadline by which each goal, objective or tactic must be completed.
- Success Criteria: List how you will be able to identify your success.

Action	Resources	Time Allocated	Deadline	Success Criteria
Identify, prioritize and list goals, objectives and tactics	List the Resources required to achieve each action	Clearly define how long each step should take to complete	Set a deadline by which each step must be completed	List how you will be able to identify your success

80

Action	Resources	Time Allocated	Deadline	Success Criteria
Identify, prioritize and list goals, objectives and tactics	List the Resources required to achieve each action	Clearly define how long each step should take to complete	Set a deadline by which each step must be completed	List how you will be able to identify your success

Action	Resources	Time Allocated	Deadline	Success Criteria
Identify, prioritise and list goals, objectives and tactics	List the Resources required to achieve each action	Clearly define how long each step should take to complete	Set a deadline by which each step must be completed	List how you will be able to identify your success

HOW DO YOU DEAL WITH PEOPLE

In order to effectively deal with your target
demographic, you must first know your personality and how
you prefer to deal with others. Your personality is an internal
factor. It is the actions you take and decisions you make. In
a room full of people, are you quick to speak, do you scan

the crowd for a familiar face or do you stand alone in a corner, anxious because of the number of people present? Are you a patient person or do you want things right now?

You will need to tailor your personality depending on your brand and what you are offering (product, sevice). If you are an introvert, but your brand requires you to interact with a large number of people, you would need to complete certain actions to get out of your shell a little more. You don't want your personality to be the one quality that holds your brand back.

Does your brand require a lot of face to face interaction with people?
In a room full of people, what is the first thing you do?

What is your biggest fears in front or as a part of a large crowd?

Are you an:

- □ Introvert: a person who usually desires to be alone or avoids social events because they feel their energy is drained by dealing with a large group of people. Shyness is not the only quality that an introvert has; it is someone who tends to avoid situations where they have to interact one on one with a group of people. For example, they attend parties but not to meet people. They typically feel alone in a crowd. Most people are not aware that tyey are introverts, visit www.dolcebelletto.com/introverts.htm for an article from Huffington Post to see if you have introvert qualities.
- □ Extrovert: an extrovert is a person who thrives in social settings; thought to be extremely confident and

a 'people person'. They are perceived as engaging and focused on more external things. Extroverts feel bored when alone and typically complete more work when working with a group.

□ Socially impassive: a person who is neither, wholly, an introvert or extrovert.

From this, you are able to determine your strengths and weaknesses, personality wise, when dealing with your market. If your personality does not match your offering, write some things that you should keep in mind when dealing with you market. For example, if you are introverted and your offering consists of you dealing one on one with a room full of people or if you are extroverted and your offering consists of you having to complete a lot of work alone, write out points and things to keep in mind to make your brand more solid and make your dealings with your market superior.

What do you need to work on so that your personality, brand and offering are on one accord?

SOCIAL MEDIA

Social media is the online presence of a person, company or brand. There are several social media networks and each one has a specific demographic that uses them more so than the others. Below is a brief description, demographic breakdown and instructions on how to set up an account and choose a user ID for the three most popular online based social media networks. *Note: When using social media as a business or to obtain business, avoid setting your page to private. This prohibits views and many people will not request to be approved. It will hurt you more than help you. Also, provide links and contact information on your pages; this ensures that you are easily accessible.*

TWITTER:

- **What is Twitter?** Twitter is a microblogging social media network that allows users to accumulate followers. You post statuses and updates called tweets that are limited to a maximum character count of 140.

- **What demographic uses Twitter?**

Twitter users

Among online adults, the % who use Twitter

	Use Twitter
All internet users (n= 1,445)	18%
a **Men** (n= 734)	17
b **Women** (n= 711)	18
a **White, Non-Hispanic** (n= 1,025)	16
b **Black, Non-Hispanic** (n= 138)	29[ac]
c **Hispanic** (n= 169)	16
a **18-29** (n= 267)	31[bcd]
b **30-49** (n= 473)	19[cd]
c **50-64** (n= 401)	9
d **65+** (n= 278)	5
a **High school grad or less** (n= 385)	17
b **Some college** (n= 433)	18
c **College+** (n= 619)	18
a **Less than $30,000/yr** (n= 328)	17
b **$30,000-$49,999** (n= 259)	18
c **$50,000-$74,999** (n= 187)	15
d **$75,000+** (n= 486)	19
a **Urban** (n= 479)	18[c]
b **Suburban** (n= 700)	19[c]
c **Rural** (n= 266)	11

Pew Research Center's Internet Project August Tracking Survey, August 07 –September 16, 2013. N=1,445 internet users ages 18+. Interviews were conducted in English and Spanish and on landline and cell phones. The margin of error for results based on all internet users is +/- 2.9 percentage points.

Note: Percentages marked with a superscript letter (e.g., [a]) indicate a statistically significant difference between that row and the row designated by that superscript letter, among categories of each demographic characteristic (e.g., age).

PEW RESEARCH CENTER

- **How do I set up a Twitter account and what name should I use?** To set up a Twitter account, visit **www.twitter.com** and click the sign up button. You will prompted to fill out an account profile which includes an image, your profile name, user tag, a short 160 character bio, location and a website. Your image could be a personal picture (refrain from one that shows obscene or offensive gestures, is pixelated or blurry or too small) or your logo. As for your user tag, choose one that is spelled correctly and uses the same spelling as your website, business name or user ID on other social media. For example, Dolcé Belletto's twitter name is @dolcebelletto which is consistent with our Instagram, Racebook and website pages. If that is not an option, try adding "official", "the", or "_" to your username.
- **How do I get a following on Twitter?** Begin by following other people in your industry and retweeting (RT) their tweets and statuses. Also, search hashtags (#)

related to what you do and your passions and engage in conversation with people there. For every self promotion tweet, post 10 tweets that support others in your industry. You don't want a me, me, me type timeline.

FACEBOOK:

- **What is Facebook?** Facebook is a social network that allows its users to create profiles and obtain up to 5,000 friends. You can post statuses, pictures and videos to share with your 'friends', create and join groups, post event invitations and information and like businesses, movements and celebrities.
- **What is a Facebook Business Page:** A Facebook business page is a profile made for a business or person. There is no maximum number of people that can like your business page and it is completely separate from your personal page.

Facebook users

Among online adults, the % who use Facebook

	Use Facebook
All internet users (n= 1,445)	71%
a Men (n= 734)	66
b Women (n= 711)	76[a]
a White, Non-Hispanic (n= 1,025)	71
b Black, Non-Hispanic (n= 138)	76
c Hispanic (n= 169)	73
a 18-29 (n= 267)	84[cd]
b 30-49 (n= 473)	79[cd]
c 50-64 (n= 401)	60[d]
d 65+ (n= 278)	45
a High school grad or less (n= 385)	71
b Some college (n= 433)	75[c]
c College+ (n= 619)	68
a Less than $30,000/yr (n= 328)	76[d]
b $30,000-$49,999 (n= 259)	76
c $50,000-$74,999 (n= 187)	68
d $75,000+ (n= 486)	69
a Urban (n= 479)	75
b Suburban (n= 700)	69
c Rural (n= 266)	71

Pew Research Center's Internet Project August Tracking Survey, August 07 –September 16, 2013. N=1,445 internet users ages 18+. Interviews were conducted in English and Spanish and on landline and cell phones. The margin of error for results based on all internet users is +/- 2.9 percentage points.

Note: Percentages marked with a superscript letter (e.g., [a]) indicate a statistically significant difference between that row and the row designated by that superscript letter, among categories of each demographic characteristic (e.g., age).

PEW RESEARCH CENTER

- **How do I set up a Facebook business page?** In order to set up a Facebook business page, you must have a personal Facebook page. To set up a Facebook profile, visit **www.facebook.com** and sign up with a valid email address. After this step, you will be prompted to complete your profile which includes an image, a profile cover image and basic information about you. After that is completed, visit **https://www.facebook.com/pages/create.php** to create your business page. There are several articles and pieces of information on the internet that explains how to customize your page by adding apps, widgets and unique features.

- **How do I get a following on my Facebook business page?** Use hashtags and post often. Engaging post increase your likes. Also, host contests or giveaways and promote your page on your website and other social media pages. Share industry news and events, as well as other happenings in the world on your

Facebook business page. This increases the number of searches that your page is likely to pop up on in search engines. You may also offer a special or reward for the person who refers the most people to your page.

- **Facebook Groups:** You can also host and create open or closed groups for people that have similar interest as you. Facebook users tend to post in groups to promote their projects and share group postings on their timeline. It isn't a necessity, but it is an option.

LINKEDIN:

- **What is LinkedIn?** LinkedIn is a professional social network that allows you to connect with other professionals around the world. While you can create business pages, LinkedIn users typically only focus on creating personal profiles.

- What demographic uses LinkedIn?

LinkedIn users

Among online adults, the % who use LinkedIn

	Use LinkedIn
All internet users(n= 1,445)	22%
a Men (n= 734)	24[b]
b Women (n= 711)	19
a White, Non-Hispanic (n= 1,025)	22[c]
b Black, Non-Hispanic (n= 138)	30[c]
c Hispanic (n= 169)	13
a 18-29 (n= 267)	15
b 30-49 (n= 473)	27[ad]
c 50-64 (n= 401)	24[ad]
d 65+ (n= 278)	13
a High school grad or less (n= 385)	12
b Some college (n= 433)	16
c College+ (n= 619)	38[ab]
a Less than $30,000/yr (n= 328)	12
b $30,000-$49,999 (n= 259)	13
c $50,000-$74,999 (n= 187)	22[ab]
d $75,000+ (n= 486)	38[abc]
a Employed (n= 912)	27[b]
b Not employed (n= 524)	12
a Urban (n= 479)	23[c]
b Suburban (n= 700)	26[c]
c Rural (n= 266)	8

Pew Research Center's Internet Project August Tracking Survey, August 07 –September 16, 2013. N=1,445 internet users ages 18+. Interviews were conducted in English and Spanish and on landline and cell phones. The margin of error for results based on all internet users is +/- 2.9 percentage points.
Note: Percentages marked with a superscript letter (e.g., [a]) indicate a statistically significant difference between that row and the row designated by that superscript letter, among categories of each demographic characteristic (e.g., age).

PEW RESEARCH CENTER

- **How do I set up a LinkedIn account?**
  Visit **www.linkedin.com** and click the join today button. You will be sent to a page where you will enter your first and last name, as well as an email address and password. From there, you will be able to fill out your profile which includes an image, basic information about you, areas of skill and your résumé.

- **How do I get a following on LinkedIn?**
  Your LinkedIn connections grow by inviting other professionals to connect or by being invited to connect. You can search for people by their job title, name or company affiliation.

WEBSITE

A website is definitely needed regardless of your offering. This allows people to find all your information in one place. It should be visually appealing and simple to navigate. People are more inclined to visit another website if they feel lost while browsing your page. Your website should have at least three tabs/pages: about, product/service and contact us, as well as links to your social media pages. Many people choose to include tabs for their blog and merchandise; these are both optional. Blogging is a time consuming activity that can help in your recognized level of expertise.

When publishing a website, buy a domain that is the correct spelling of your business name, check your website for spelling and grammatical errors and buy a hosting plan that includes email addresses.

Website URL:
Tabs ☐ About: a page that features your biography or company history and an image. ☐ Product/Service: a page that features your service(s) list, images/samples of your product, more information on what you are offering to the market ☐ Contact Us: a page that features your contact information. ☐ Blog (optional) ☐ Shop/Merchandise (optional) *These are all in addition to your home page, which most people use to show their logo and tagline.*

Chapter 6:

Developing Your Image

"...if you project the image you wish the world to see, eventually it will become reality."

— *Tera Lynn Childs*

DEVELOPING YOUR IMAGE

Now that we have broken down your brand and gotten a clearer understanding of what makes up your brand and who is in your target market, it is time to develop your visual presentation/image. In this chapter, you will complete activities to determine the best colors that work for you, what is appealing to your target market and figure out how to tie a unique image into your brand and offering.

COLOR ANALYSIS

SKIN TONE

It is important to determine the tone of your skin. Are you warm or cool? Once that is known, it is easy to pick out colors that look the best on your skin. Complete the table below:

	Warm	Cool
Eyes	Brown, amber or hazel	Blue, gray or green
Hair	Strawberry blond, red, black or brown Undertones: gold, red, orange or yellow	Blond, brown or black Undertones: blue, silver, violet or ash
Veins (their appearance under the skin)	More green looking	More blue looking
Neutral Shades	More flattering in off-white & tan	More flattering in pure white& black
Sun's Affect	Gold brown tan	Burn then tan

If you feel like your balance is in between the two, then you are classified as having neutral undertones.

There are certain colors that complement skin tones:
- Warm skin tone:
  - Richer toned colors complement the undertones in your skin better. Examples: Cranberries, plums, hunter green, tans and rust oranges.
- Cool Skin Tone
  - Truer toned colors complement the undertones of the skin. Examples: royal blue, purple, lilac and green.

DEVELOPING AN AUTHENTIC STYLE

When creating your style for your image, you need to take into consideration your demographic, body shape and what you feel comfortable in. This style should be able to translate from event to event, outfit to outfit and carry the same message at all times.

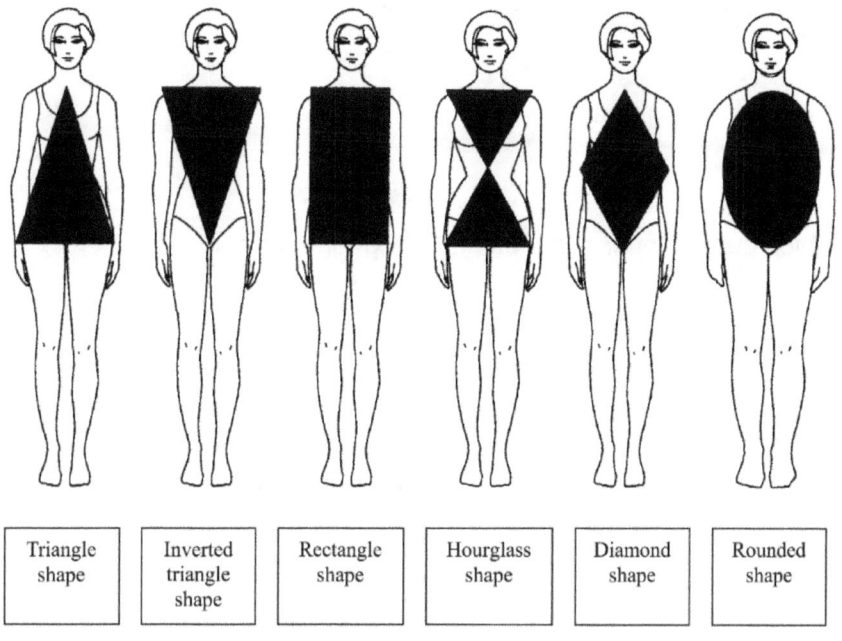

| Triangle shape | Inverted triangle shape | Rectangle shape | Hourglass shape | Diamond shape | Rounded shape |

Female Body Shapes

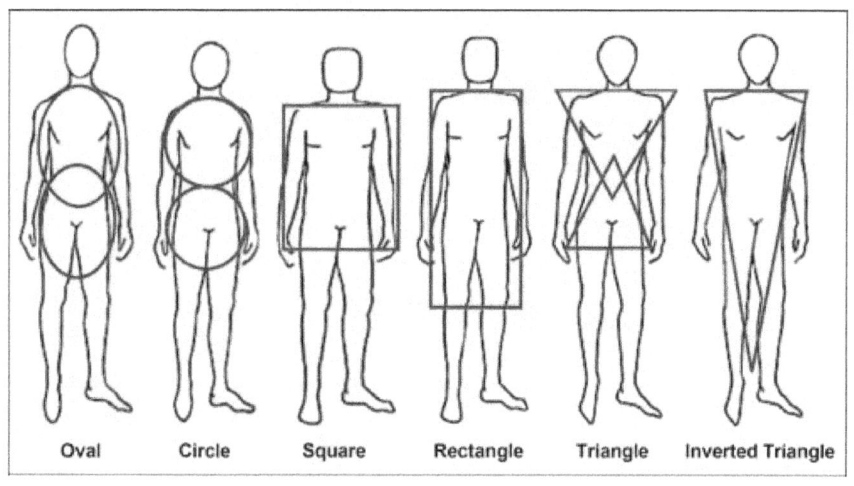

Oval — Circle — Square — Rectangle — Triangle — Inverted Triangle

Male Body Shapes

What is your body shape?

Which cut of clothing is most flattering for your body type?

What kind of image do you feel is necessary to have in order to keep your message clear and your trifecta cohesive?

What does your demographic find appealing or is visually drawn to?

Whose style do you see your demographic emulating?

What type of clothing makes you uncomfortable?

What type of clothing are you most comfortable in?

What are most people wearing in your industry?

What elements of your clothing are always unique?

What part of your image do you want to stand out?

Craft your style:

☐ Casual:

☐ Night Out:

☐ Formal Event:

☐ Professional:

The biggest part about your image is your ability to pull it off. If your unique quality is pastel colored hair, then you must be able to walk into an event confidently every time with that pastel colored hair. If you do not appear confident or are constantly pulling at your clothing, your message and solidity of your trifecta is lost in the insecurity you are exuding.

Consulting an image consultant and stylist are definite ways to construct an authentic style that is comfortably and genuinely you. Find one who is knowledgeable about your industry!

Chapter 7:

Do I Need a Team?

"I love teamwork. I love the idea of

everyone rallying together to help

me win.   "

— Jarod Kintz

DO I NEED A TEAM?

A team is a group of people joined together with a common goal in mind. Each teammate usually has their own strength(s) that benefits the team as a whole. Based on that definition, the short answer is yes, you need a team. Who your team consists of is based solely on what you are seeking to accomplish; however, I have provided a list of team members that you should have.

- Brand Strategist: a professional who has a background in brand development and brand management. They specialize in developing a brand for their client that will boost awareness, following, loyalty and revenue.

- Graphic Designer: a professional who puts together images, text and composition to form a design. Graphic designers can aid with your brand identity visual products; i.e. - logo, business cards, brochures, fliers, social media backgrounds, banners and posters. They can also help design your website. Using a graphic designer gives your material and items a professional look which increases your value.

- Hair Stylist/ Barber: a professionally trained person who styles, cuts and trims your hair. Barbers and hair stylist keep up with hair trends and are able to assist you in maintaining a professional appearance.

- Image Consultant: a professional who works with clients on their visual appearance. Includes clothing, etiquette, styling, as well as verbal and non-verbal communication.
- Lawyer/ Legal Analyst: a professional with a strong background in law, negotiations, contracts and the legalities of business. It is EXTREMELY necessary to have a lawyer on your team to ensure that your business dealings are of good faith and intent. This also prevents you from entering into contracts or agreements that do not benefit you.
- Makeup Artist: a professional trained in applying cosmetics to the face and body. When hiring a makeup artist, hire a professional with experience and a portfolio. You typically use one for professionally shot material (video, film, photo, television) and major events.
- Manager/Agent: a professional who guides your career in your industry. They can negotiate contracts, book jobs, establish a

budget and hire a team to work with you among other things. This team mate helps alleviate some of the pressures and stress on their client.

- Marketing Director: a professional that develops and implements a marketing plan/ strategy tailored to your demographic. This plan typically includes promotions of some type and advertising.

- Photographer/ Videographer: a professional with a background in editing software, lighting and the proper use of a camera. They provide professionally edited and shot images and videos for your website, social media, press kit and any other items that require pictures and media.

- Publicist: a professional who generates and maintains public awareness and interest about their client; they are the bridge between the press/media and their client. They also deal in crisis management and aversion in the case that you are caught in a scandal.

As the saying goes, you are only as strong as the weakest member of your team, so be sure to research the professionals you choose. Find a team that believes in your vision and goals as much as you do so that they are enthusiastic about your projects! Use social media and Google to find professionals in your area. A lot of professionals hashtag themselves and their businesses. Contact them and schedule a time to sit down and discuss your brand with them and your expectations. Putting a team in place helps you in areas that you may feel unsure about and gives you extra feedback on what you are doing and if you are headed in the right direction.

Teammate	Name &Contact	Budget Remember to note the frequency (per month, per week, etc.)
Brand Strategist		
Graphic Designer		
Hair Stylist/Barber		

Image Consultant		
Lawyer/Legal Analyst		
Makeup Artist		
Manager		
Marketing Director		
Photographer/ Videographer		
Publicist		

Chapter 8:

Summary

"Change is a process, not an event."

SUMMARY

You just spent seven chapters reading and
completing the first steps to developing a plan to create or
change your brand and image. Chances are there are a lot
of new things you will put in place and some areas you may
not feel comfortable about just yet; and that is fine. By
purchasing this book, you have taken the initiative and
shown that you are open to change. Along with that
mindset, though, you must also remain open to receiving
feedback from those around you. There are some people in
the world whose only intent is to dissuade and dishearten
you; but you have some people who really want to see you

succeed. Try to surround yourself with those types of people and always remember that their words are not meant to hurt you, but to motivate you and keep you headed in the right direction.

Your trifecta (brand, image and offering {product, service, career, profession, talent or art}) is the building block you need to develop success. It is important to take the time to plan and strategize so that your foundation is a strong and stable one. Nurture your brand and your image the way you nurture your offering and watch them bloom together. This plan is not going to get you to your goals overnight. You must be remain realistic and understand that this is a process and it is not instantaneous. Assess your action plan as you complete it to make sure that you are still on the right path and to make sure that you are not taking huge steps backwards or running in place!

And remember,
Success is just around the corner!
Well Wishes,
Contrecia T. Tharpe

Notes:_____

_____

_____

_____

_____

_____

_____

_____

_____

_____

_____

_____

_____

_____

_____

_____

_____

_____

_____

_____

Notes:_____

_____

_____

_____

_____

_____

_____

_____

_____

_____

_____

_____

_____

_____

_____

_____

_____

_____

_____

_____

Notes:_____

_____

_____

_____

_____

_____

_____

_____

_____

_____

_____

_____

_____

_____

_____

_____

_____

_____

_____

Notes:_____

_____

_____

_____

_____

_____

_____

_____

_____

_____

_____

_____

_____

_____

_____

_____

_____

_____

_____

_____

_____

_____

Notes:_____

_____

_____

_____

_____

_____

_____

_____

_____

_____

_____

_____

_____

_____

_____

_____

_____

_____

_____

Notes:_____

_____

_____

_____

_____

_____

_____

_____

_____

_____

_____

_____

_____

_____

_____

_____

_____

_____

_____

_____

_____

Notes:_____

_____

_____

_____

_____

_____

_____

_____

_____

_____

_____

_____

_____

_____

_____

_____

_____

_____

_____

_____

_____

Notes:_____

_____

_____

_____

_____

_____

_____

_____

_____

_____

_____

_____

_____

_____

_____

_____

_____

_____

_____

Notes:_____

_____

_____

_____

_____

_____

_____

_____

_____

_____

_____

_____

_____

_____

_____

_____

_____

_____

_____

_____

_____

_____

Notes:_____

_____

_____

_____

_____

_____

_____

_____

_____

_____

_____

_____

_____

_____

_____

_____

_____

_____

_____

_____

_____

_____

Notes:_____

_____

_____

_____

_____

_____

_____

_____

_____

_____

_____

_____

_____

_____

_____

_____

_____

_____

_____

Notes:_____

_____

_____

_____

_____

_____

_____

_____

_____

_____

_____

_____

_____

_____

_____

_____

_____

_____

_____

_____